Shadows of Hunger

Unraveling the Mind in Eating Disorders

Freudian Trips

Copyright Page

© 2023 by Freudian Trips

All rights reserved. No part of this book may be reproduced in any form or by any electronic or mechanical means, including information storage and retrieval systems, without permission in writing from the publisher, except by a reviewer who may quote brief passages in a review.

This book is a work of non-fiction. Unless otherwise noted, the author and the publisher make no explicit guarantees as to the accuracy of the information contained in this book and will not be held responsible for any errors or omissions.

Published by Omniterra Media Inc

First Edition

Visit the author's website at www.freudiantrips.com

Disclaimer

The views and opinions expressed in this book are those of the author(s) and do not necessarily reflect the official policy or position of any other agency, organization, employer, or company. The contents of this book are for informational and educational purposes only and are not intended to serve as professional advice, diagnosis, or treatment.

The information provided in this book is believed to be accurate and reliable as of the date of publication. However, it may include some errors or inaccuracies, and no warranty or guarantee is provided regarding the accuracy, timeliness, or applicability of the content.

Readers are encouraged to consult with professional philosophers, educators, or other qualified professionals where appropriate for personalized advice. The author(s) and publisher shall not be liable for any loss, damage, or harm caused or alleged to be caused, directly or indirectly, by the information or ideas contained, suggested, or referenced in this book.

By reading this book, the reader acknowledges and agrees that they are solely responsible for how they interpret and apply the information contained herein.

This book may also include references to other works, studies, and sources. These references are provided for further reading and exploration and do not imply endorsement or validation of the specific theories, viewpoints, or interpretations presented in those works.

Introduction: Unveiling the Shadows of Hunger

Eating disorders (Eds) are complex and often misunderstood conditions that affect people's relationship with food and their bodies. Imagine your mind constantly occupied with thoughts about food, weight, and body image, often to the detriment of health, happiness, and daily functioning. This is the reality for millions worldwide struggling with Eds. These disorders are not mere choices or phases; they are serious mental health conditions that require understanding, compassion, and effective treatment.

Understanding Eating Disorders: More Than Just Food

Eating disorders, including anorexia nervosa, bulimia nervosa, and binge eating disorder, manifest in different ways. Some individuals may severely restrict their food intake, while others might eat large amounts in a short period, often followed by feelings of guilt or attempts to counteract the binge. What's common among these conditions is an intense preoccupation with body weight, shape, and food, leading to harmful eating behaviors and significant distress.

While the physical consequences of Eds, like malnutrition or weight fluctuations, are often visible, the psychological aspects are less apparent but equally crucial. These disorders are deeply entwined with one's emotions, self-perception, and mental well-being. They can stem from various factors, including low self-esteem, perfectionism, trauma, and societal pressures, forming a complex web that traps the individual in unhealthy patterns.

The Significance of Understanding the Psychological Aspects

To effectively address eating disorders, we must delve into the psychological realm. Understanding the 'why' behind these disorders helps us empathize with those affected and develop more effective, compassionate treatment approaches. It's not just about encouraging someone to eat more or less; it's about addressing the underlying emotional and cognitive factors that drive their behaviors.

Psychological understanding also helps break down stigma and misconceptions surrounding Eds. By illuminating the mental and emotional struggles involved, we foster a more supportive environment for those affected, encouraging them to seek help and speak openly about their experiences.

Objectives of This Book

This book aims to shed light on the intricate psychological landscape of eating disorders. We will explore:

Different Types of Eating Disorders: Understanding their unique characteristics and how they impact individuals.

Psychological Foundations: Delving into the mental and emotional factors contributing to the development and maintenance of EDs.

Personal Narratives: Sharing stories from those who have battled these disorders, offering insight into their experiences.

Treatment and Healing: Exploring various therapeutic approaches and strategies for recovery.

Our journey through this book is not just an academic exploration but an empathetic one. We aim to connect with the hearts and minds of those touched by eating disorders, whether personally or through a loved one, and to offer hope, understanding, and pathways to healing. Join us as we unveil the shadows of hunger and illuminate the path to a deeper comprehension and a more compassionate response to eating disorders.

Chapter 1: The Many Faces of Eating Disorders

Welcome to a journey through the world of eating disorders (Eds), a realm often shrouded in mystery and misunderstanding. In this chapter, we'll explore the different types of Eds, their symptoms, and who they typically affect. Think of this as a map, guiding you through a landscape where each disorder has its own terrain, with unique signs and landmarks.

Understanding the Types of Eating Disorders

Anorexia Nervosa: Picture a person who is deeply afraid of gaining weight, so much so that they limit their food intake drastically. They might see themselves as overweight, even if they are underweight. This fear of weight gain drives them to eat very little, often leading to significant weight loss.

Bulimia Nervosa: Now, imagine someone who experiences episodes where they eat an unusually large amount of food in one sitting (bingeing) and then tries to compensate for this overeating. They might induce vomiting, exercise excessively, or use laxatives (purging). This cycle of bingeing and purging becomes a distressing pattern.

Binge Eating Disorder: Here, individuals regularly eat large amounts of food, feeling a loss of control during these episodes. Unlike bulimia, they do not regularly use purging methods afterward. These binge episodes often lead to feelings of shame, distress, or guilt.

Other Specified Feeding or Eating Disorders: This category includes disorders that don't neatly fit into the other definitions but are still serious. For example, someone might have symptoms of anorexia but still maintain a normal weight, or they might purge without bingeing.

Recognizing the Symptoms

While each disorder has its unique symptoms, there are common signs to look out for:

Drastic changes in weight (loss or gain)

Preoccupation with food, dieting, and body image

Unusual eating habits (like eating alone, skipping meals, or avoiding certain foods)

Emotional distress, particularly around meals

In cases of bulimia and binge eating, secretive behavior regarding food

Who Gets Eating Disorders? Prevalence and Demographics

Eating disorders can affect anyone, regardless of age, gender, or background, but certain patterns have been observed:

Anorexia and Bulimia: Primarily affect adolescents and young adults, with a higher prevalence among females. However, they can occur at any age and also affect males.

Binge Eating Disorder: Tends to start in the late teens or early 20s but can occur later in life as well. It's more evenly distributed between genders compared to anorexia and bulimia.

Cultural Influences: While EDs are seen worldwide, they are more prevalent in societies where thinness is highly valued.

A Diverse Spectrum

Eating disorders are not just about food; they are complex conditions influenced by a mix of biological, psychological, and cultural factors. They can look different in each person, which is why understanding these disorders is so crucial. In the next chapters, we'll delve deeper into what drives these disorders and how they can be treated. Remember, behind every eating disorder, there's a human face, a story, and a path towards healing.

Chapter 2: The Inner Workings: Psychological Foundations of Eating Disorders

In this chapter, we delve into the psychological underpinnings of eating disorders (Eds). Imagine the mind as a garden, where various seeds—thoughts, experiences, and emotions—can grow into either healthy plants or harmful weeds. Understanding the psychological aspects of Eds is like learning how to nurture this garden, recognizing what causes the harmful weeds to grow and how to cultivate healthier, more resilient plants.

Unraveling the Mystery: Psychological Theories Explaining Eds

Cognitive-Behavioral Perspective: This theory suggests that how we think (cognitive) and how we act (behavioral) play a critical role in EDs. For example, if someone believes they must be thin to be accepted (a cognitive aspect), they might resort to harmful eating behaviors (a behavioral aspect).

Psychodynamic Approach: Rooted in the ideas of early psychology, this approach looks at how past experiences, especially in childhood, shape our self-image and behaviors. It suggests that EDs might be a way to cope with unresolved emotional issues.

Sociocultural Factors: This theory emphasizes the role of society and culture in shaping our views about body image and attractiveness. The pressure to meet certain beauty standards can lead to distorted body image and unhealthy eating habits.

The Role of Self-Esteem, Body Image, and Control

Self-Esteem: How we view and value ourselves profoundly affects our eating behaviors. Low self-esteem might lead someone to believe that they need to change their body to be worthy or accepted.

Body Image: This is how we perceive our physical appearance. A negative body image might make someone more prone to developing an ED, as they constantly strive to change their body to fit an ideal that may not be realistic or healthy.

Control: For some, controlling their food intake or body weight is a way to cope with feelings of helplessness or chaos in other areas of their life. It can be a misguided attempt to exert control when other parts of their life feel uncontrollable.

The Impact of Trauma and Past Experiences

Trauma, whether emotional, physical, or psychological, can leave deep imprints on our psyche. For some individuals, EDs may develop as a way to cope with or exert control over the pain of these experiences. Past traumas, particularly those involving body image or self-esteem, can significantly influence one's relationship with food and their body.

A Complex Tapestry

Eating disorders are not simply about food; they are complex conditions woven from many psychological threads. Understanding these disorders requires us to look beyond the surface behaviors and explore the deeper psychological roots. Recognizing the role of thoughts, feelings, and past experiences can help us empathize with those suffering from EDs and guide them towards healthier mental and emotional landscapes. In the next chapter, we will explore how these internal struggles are influenced by the world around us—the social dimension of eating disorders.

Chapter 3: The World Around Us: The Social Dimension of Eating Disorders

In this chapter, we turn our focus outward, exploring how our social environment influences eating disorders (EDs). Think of society as a large mirror reflecting back at us images, ideas, and norms about how we should look and behave. This mirror, along with our closest relationships, can significantly shape our relationship with food and our bodies.

The Influence of Media and Societal Standards

Media Impact: Daily, we're bombarded with images in movies, TV shows, magazines, and online platforms showcasing idealized body types. Often, these bodies are unrealistically thin or muscular, creating an impression that this is the norm we should all strive to achieve. This constant exposure can distort our body image and fuel dissatisfaction and harmful eating behaviors.

Social Media and Comparison: Social media platforms are ripe grounds for comparing our bodies to others. Here, edited and filtered images present an illusion of 'perfection' that is hard to achieve in real life. This constant comparison can lead to feelings of inadequacy and a distorted perception of our own bodies.

Societal Standards and Expectations: Society often has set ideas about what is 'beautiful' or 'desirable,' which can vary across cultures and change over time. These standards can put immense pressure on individuals to conform, particularly on those who feel they don't naturally fit these expectations.

Family Dynamics and Peer Pressure

Family Influences: Our family's attitudes towards food, body image, and health can significantly impact our own. Comments about weight, dieting habits of family members, or even family meal patterns can influence our relationship with food and body image.

Peer Pressure: Especially during adolescent years, the desire to fit in with friends can be overwhelming. This can lead to adopting unhealthy eating habits or attitudes towards one's body if they're prevalent in one's social circle.

Cultural and Gender-Specific Aspects

Cultural Factors: Different cultures have varying ideals of beauty and body size. In some cultures, being 'thin' is seen as desirable, while in others, a fuller figure might be preferred. These cultural ideals can impact how individuals view their bodies and their risk of developing an ED.

Gender-Specific Issues: While EDs can affect anyone, regardless of gender, societal expectations around masculinity and femininity can play a role. For instance, women might feel pressure to be thin, while men might feel the need to be more muscular.

However, it's essential to note that EDs are increasingly being recognized and reported among all genders.

Navigating the Social Landscape

Understanding the social dimension of EDs helps us see how our environment can both trigger and perpetuate these disorders. It also highlights the importance of fostering a more inclusive, realistic portrayal of body types in media and society. As we move forward, we'll see how these external pressures intertwine with our internal psychological world, creating a complex web that individuals with EDs navigate daily. The next chapter will dive deeper into the biological aspects, adding another layer to our understanding of these multifaceted disorders.

Chapter 4: The Body's Language: The Biology of Behavior in Eating Disorders

In this chapter, we'll explore how the complex machinery of our bodies – our genes, brain, and hormones – can influence eating disorders (EDs). Imagine your body as an intricate network, with each part sending and receiving messages that affect how you think, feel, and behave around food.

Neurological and Genetic Factors in Eds

The Brain's Role: Our brain is the control center for how we think, feel, and act. In people with EDs, certain areas of the brain that regulate appetite, mood, and reward may function differently. This can affect how they perceive hunger, fullness, and satisfaction from eating.

Genetic Influences: Just like we inherit physical traits from our parents, we can also inherit biological predispositions to certain conditions, including EDs. Studies show that if a close family member has an ED, the risk of developing one is higher. This doesn't mean it's certain, but there's a genetic vulnerability.

The Role of Hormones and Neurotransmitters

Hormones: These are chemicals in our body that act like messengers. Hormones related to hunger (like ghrelin) and fullness (like leptin) can influence eating behaviors. Sometimes, in people with EDs, these messages might not be processed normally, leading to disordered eating patterns.

Neurotransmitters: These are the brain's chemical messengers. They play a role in mood and emotion. For example, serotonin is linked to feelings of well-being and happiness. Imbalances in neurotransmitters can influence mood and are often associated with EDs, affecting how someone might relate to food and body image.

Understanding the Brain-Gut Connection

The 'brain-gut axis' is a two-way communication system between your brain and your digestive system. This connection means that your gut health can affect your mental state and vice versa. For instance, the feeling of stress might upset your stomach, or a gut issue might affect your mood. In EDs, this complex relationship can be disrupted, affecting how you experience hunger, fullness, and the emotional aspects of eating.

A Symphony of Signals

The biological aspect of EDs is like a symphony, with each part of the body playing a specific role, and sometimes the music doesn't sound as it should. Understanding these biological factors helps in comprehending why EDs are not simply a matter of choice or willpower but involve deeper, underlying biological processes. As we continue our journey, we will see how these biological aspects intertwine with psychological and social elements, forming the multifaceted experience of EDs. In the next chapter, we will explore the personal experiences of those battling EDs, adding a human touch to our understanding.

Chapter 5: Voices in the Silence: Personal Struggles with Eating Disorders

In this chapter, we step into the shoes of those who have experienced eating disorders (Eds) firsthand. Through their stories, we gain a deeper, more personal understanding of these conditions. It's like listening to a chorus of voices, each sharing a unique yet interconnected tale.

Personal Narratives and Hypothetical Case Studies

Anna's Story (Anorexia Nervosa): Anna, a high school student, began avoiding meals and obsessively counting calories. Initially praised for losing weight, she soon became trapped in a cycle of severe restriction, driven by a fear of gaining weight and a distorted self-image.

Ben's Journey (Binge Eating Disorder): Ben, a middle-aged office worker, struggled with episodes of eating large amounts of food in secret, often at night. Feelings of shame and guilt followed these binges, yet he felt unable to control them.

Clara's Battle (Bulimia Nervosa): Clara, a college athlete, found herself in a cycle of bingeing on food and then purging through excessive exercise and occasional vomiting. While maintaining a normal weight, she suffered in silence, fearing judgment.

Each story illustrates the diverse ways Eds can manifest and affect individuals' lives.

The Hidden Struggle: Stigma and Secrecy

Many with EDs suffer in silence, hidden behind a veil of secrecy. This secrecy is often fueled by stigma – a fear of being misunderstood, judged, or labeled. Stigma can lead to feelings of isolation, making it harder to seek help. It also perpetuates myths about EDs, such as they only affect certain types of people, or are simply a matter of willpower.

The Internal Dialogue of Someone with an ED

Imagine a constant, internal conversation filled with self-criticism, doubt, and fear. This is the reality for many with EDs. Thoughts like "I'm not good enough," "I must control my eating to be accepted," or "I don't deserve to eat" are common. This internal dialogue can be relentless and exhausting, influencing behaviors and perpetuating the disorder.

Breaking the Silence

Understanding these personal experiences is key to empathizing with and supporting those with EDs. It helps us see beyond the surface behaviors to the human struggle underneath. As we move forward, we will explore how these disorders coexist with other mental health conditions, adding another layer to our understanding of the complexity and challenges faced by those with EDs.

Chapter 6: Navigating the Crossroads: When Eating Disorders Coexist with Other Conditions

In this chapter, we explore the landscape where eating disorders (EDs) intersect with other mental health challenges. Imagine walking a path and coming to a crossroads where multiple roads meet. This is similar to what happens when an ED coexists with another mental health condition, creating a complex and challenging journey.

Comorbidity with Other Mental Health Disorders

Anxiety and Eds: Anxiety disorders, such as generalized anxiety or social anxiety, are often found alongside Eds. For example, the intense worry about body image or social judgment can exacerbate ED behaviors.

Depression and Eds: It's not uncommon for individuals with Eds to also experience depression. The feelings of sadness, hopelessness, and loss of interest in activities can influence eating behaviors, either through loss of appetite or using food as a form of comfort.

Obsessive-Compulsive Disorder (OCD) and Eds: Some people with Eds exhibit behaviors similar to OCD, such as obsessive thoughts about food or compulsive rituals around eating and exercise.

The Complexity of Dual Diagnoses

When someone has an ED along with another mental health condition, it's like dealing with two storms at once. Each condition can feed into and worsen the other, creating a complex situation that is challenging to untangle. For instance, the low self-esteem from an ED can deepen depression, and heightened anxiety can make ED symptoms worse.

Treatment Challenges and Strategies

Integrated Treatment Approach: Addressing both conditions simultaneously is crucial. This might involve a combination of therapies, such as cognitive-behavioral therapy for the ED and medication for depression or anxiety.

Personalized Care: Each person's experience with coexisting conditions is unique. Treatment must be tailored to address the specific combination of symptoms and their interplay.

Support Systems: Strong support systems are vital. This can include family, friends, support groups, and mental health professionals. They provide the understanding, encouragement, and accountability needed for managing multiple conditions.

Holistic Approaches: Beyond traditional treatments, holistic approaches like mindfulness, yoga, or art therapy can be beneficial. They help in managing stress, improving self-esteem, and developing healthier coping mechanisms.

Embracing the Complexity

Understanding the interplay between EDs and other mental health conditions illuminates the complexity of these experiences. By acknowledging this complexity, we can approach treatment with a more compassionate, comprehensive perspective. The next chapters will delve into healing and recovery, guiding us through the diverse strategies to support those navigating these crossroads.

Chapter 7: Pathways to Recovery: Healing Minds, Mending Bodies

In this chapter, we explore the journey towards healing from eating disorders (EDs). Imagine a road to recovery, lined with various tools and helpers, each offering a unique form of support. This road can lead to a place where the mind and body are in better harmony.

Overview of Therapeutic Approaches

Cognitive-Behavioral Therapy (CBT): This approach focuses on changing negative thought patterns and behaviors. For someone with an ED, CBT helps in recognizing and altering distorted thoughts about body image, food, and self-worth.

Family-Based Therapy (FBT): Especially effective for adolescents, this therapy involves family members in the treatment process. The family learns how to support their loved one, helping them regain control over eating in a healthy way.

Nutritional Counseling: Working with a dietitian or nutritionist can help restore a healthy relationship with food. This includes developing meal plans, learning about balanced nutrition, and understanding the body's actual needs.

The Role of Psychotherapy and Counseling

Individual Therapy: This provides a safe space for individuals to explore their emotions, experiences, and behaviors related to their ED. Therapists can offer coping strategies and emotional support tailored to each person's needs.

Group Therapy: Here, individuals can share experiences and support each other under professional guidance. Knowing others face similar struggles can be comforting and reduce feelings of isolation.

Emerging Treatments and Holistic Approaches

Medication: While there are no specific medications to cure EDs, some can help manage co-occurring conditions like depression or anxiety, which can indirectly aid in treating the ED.

Mindfulness and Meditation: These practices help in developing a better awareness of the body's hunger and fullness cues, as well as managing stress and negative emotions that might trigger ED behaviors.

Art and Movement Therapy: Activities like art, dance, or yoga encourage self-expression and body acceptance. They can be therapeutic outlets for emotions and help in reconnecting with the body in a positive way.

Experiential Therapies: These include activities like equine therapy (working with horses) or adventure therapy. They offer new experiences that build confidence, self-awareness, and coping skills in non-traditional settings.

A Multifaceted Approach to Healing

Recovering from an ED is not a one-size-fits-all process. It often requires a combination of therapies and approaches, each addressing different aspects of the disorder. The journey is personal and can be challenging, but with the right support and tools, healing and a healthier relationship with food and the body are achievable. In the next chapter, we will look beyond the individual to the role of community, education, and prevention in addressing EDs.

Chapter 8: Joining Hands: The Power of Community in Confronting Eating Disorders

In this chapter, we step beyond the individual experience to explore how communities, education, and proactive measures play vital roles in addressing eating disorders (EDs). Imagine a network of support, like a safety net, made up of different strands—family, friends, healthcare professionals, educators, and society at large—each crucial for providing support and understanding.

Community and Support Systems

Support Groups: These are spaces where individuals with EDs and their loved ones can share experiences, challenges, and successes. Knowing that others understand their journey can be incredibly validating and encouraging.

Role of Family and Friends: Loved ones can offer crucial emotional support. Understanding EDs, recognizing early warning signs, and knowing how to provide the right kind of help can make a significant difference.

Healthcare Community: Doctors, therapists, and nutritionists form a professional network that can offer comprehensive care. Collaborative treatment approaches ensure that all aspects of the ED are addressed.

The Role of Education and Awareness

In Schools and Universities: Education about EDs can start early, with programs in schools and universities. These programs can focus on promoting body positivity, healthy eating habits, and stress management skills.

Public Awareness Campaigns: Campaigns can help dispel myths about EDs, reduce stigma, and spread awareness about the signs of EDs and the importance of seeking help.

Training for Professionals: Training doctors, teachers, and counselors to recognize the signs of EDs can lead to earlier intervention and support.

Preventative Measures and Early Intervention

Promoting Positive Body Image: Encouraging acceptance and appreciation of diverse body types can counteract the societal pressures that often contribute to EDs.

Early Identification: Recognizing the early signs of an ED is crucial. This could include changes in eating habits, extreme concern with weight and body shape, or increased isolation.

Accessible Resources: Making sure information and help are easy to find and access is key. This includes hotlines, websites, and community health centers offering guidance and support.

A Collective Effort

Tackling EDs is not just about individual treatment; it's a community effort. By building a supportive environment, promoting understanding and education, and implementing early intervention strategies, we can create a society that is better equipped to prevent and address these complex disorders. In our concluding chapter, we will summarize the key insights from this book and look at future directions in the research and treatment of EDs, as well as offer a message of hope and empowerment for those affected.

Conclusion: A Journey of Understanding and Hope

As we reach the end of our exploration into the complex world of eating disorders (EDs), let's take a moment to reflect on the key insights we've gathered and look ahead to the future. This journey, though filled with challenges, is also one of resilience and hope.

Summarizing Key Insights

The Multifaceted Nature of EDs: We've seen that EDs are not just about food; they are intricate conditions influenced by psychological, social, and biological factors. Understanding these multifaceted aspects is crucial for effective treatment and support.

The Importance of Personal Stories: The narratives of those who have experienced EDs firsthand remind us that behind every disorder is a human face, a unique story, and a struggle that deserves compassion and understanding.

The Role of Community and Society: We've learned that the fight against EDs is not just an individual battle but a collective one.

Education, awareness, and a supportive community are key elements in both prevention and recovery.

The Diversity of Treatment Approaches: From psychotherapy and nutritional counseling to emerging holistic approaches, there is no one-size-fits-all solution. Recovery is a personal journey, and treatment needs to be tailored to the individual.

Future Directions in Research and Treatment

Expanding Understanding: Ongoing research is essential to deepen our understanding of EDs, especially regarding their biological and genetic underpinnings.

Innovative Treatments: The future of treatment may include more personalized approaches, integrating new technologies like virtual reality or apps for self-monitoring and support.

Prevention Strategies: Research into effective prevention methods is vital, aiming to identify and address risk factors early on.

Global Perspectives: Considering cultural differences in the manifestation and treatment of EDs can lead to more inclusive and effective global health strategies.

An Empowering Message for Those Affected

If you or someone you know is struggling with an eating disorder, remember this: Your journey is valid, and help is available. You are not defined by your disorder, and with the right support and treatment, recovery is possible. Your story doesn't end with ED; it's a part of your larger, ongoing narrative, one filled with potential for growth, healing, and hope.

This book is not just a collection of information; it's an invitation to understand, empathize, and join in the collective effort to support those facing EDs. As we close this chapter, let's carry forward the message of hope, resilience, and the belief that together, we can make a difference in the lives of those battling eating disorders.

About Freudian Trips

Welcome to Freudian Trips, your dedicated platform for diving deep into the world of psychology. We are more than just a YouTube channel or a book publisher. We are a beacon of enlightenment, making complex psychological concepts accessible and engaging for all.

Our YouTube channel is a rich repository of psychology made simple. We take the profound and often complex ideas from the world of psychology and break them down into digestible, easy-to-understand content. From the foundational theories of Freud to the cognitive insights of Piaget, we cover a broad spectrum of psychological schools and thoughts, making psychology accessible to everyone, regardless of their background or prior knowledge.

As a book publisher, we take the same approach, transforming intricate psychological theories into comprehensible narratives. Our books are not just collections of words, but vessels of wisdom that make psychology approachable and relatable. We believe that psychology should not be confined to academic circles, but should be available to all who seek to understand the human mind and behavior.

At Freudian Trips, we believe in the power of curiosity and the pursuit of knowledge. We are here to stoke the fires of your curiosity, to guide you on your intellectual journey, and to help you navigate the fascinating world of psychology.

If you are someone who is not afraid to question, to explore, and to learn, then you are in the right place. Join us on this journey of exploration, as we make psychology easy to understand, one concept at a time.

Be sure to visit our Youtube channel at: www.freudiantrips.com/youtube

You can also visit us on the web at www.freudiantrips.com

Welcome to The Freudian Trip community. Stay curious. Stay enlightened.

www.ingramcontent.com/pod-product-compliance
Lightning Source LLC
Chambersburg PA
CBHW060906260726
48661CB00008B/3495